30 Lessons in Love, Leadership, and Legacy from Harriet Tubman

Workbook

Karol V. Brown

30 Lessons in Love, Leadership, and Legacy from Harriet Tubman Workbook

Copyright © 2012 by Karol V. Brown

ISBN 978-0-9840050-2-4

Date: _____

This Workbook belongs to: _____

Forward

This workbook is for you to write down your thoughts.
I am sure that,

30 Lessons in Love, Leadership and Legacy from

Harriet Tubman

will give you something to think about.

Take your time and remember, Keep on Going!

Karol

PART ONE: LEARN FROM THE PAST

Lesson 1: The Spirit of a Leader

Hold on to pleasant thoughts. **Appreciate the family time. Keep your faith, and don't let anyone take yourself-esteem.**

Harriet Tubman's childhood was not one that would be encouraging to a child. She suffered from physical and mental abuse. However, she had something to hold on to when there was no one around to protect her. When there is nothing else to hold on to, there is love of family and faith in God. People can't allow a hard life to break their spirits. This strong spirit is part of one's personality. With many people, the spirit is within them, but their time to develop it just has not yet come. Hold on to your spirit; your time is coming.

Discussion questions:

When times are hard and your spirit is down, what do you have to hold on to?

_____

_____

_____

_____

_____

_____

_____

What are some times you have fond memories of?

What do you think of your own self-esteem? Is this an area you need help with?

Lesson 2: Overcome Negative Past Experiences

Lesson Learned: Humility and endurance are survival skills

Minty felt like a neglected weed. How lonely and unimportant she must have felt to think of herself as a weed. A neglected weed is an unwanted plant, no attention or caring for its life. People do not allow weeds in their garden to grow freely and strong.

They stop them as soon as they start to develop. If you water and fertilize the garden, you don't waste any water on the weeds. It's left to die. In our program, my husband sings the Negro Spiritual, "Motherless Child." I can imagine Minty singing this to herself. The songs were in her minds and hearts. Freedom begins in the mind. To overcome negative experiences, you have to free your mind of any bitterness. Forgiveness frees the mind and brings peace. This is the first step to overcoming the past.

Discussion questions:

Are you harboring unforgiveness toward someone who has wronged you? Are you ready and willing to forgive that person to help yourself?

_____

_____

_____

_____

_____

_____

How does Harriet Tubman's story help you understand how forgiveness will help you overcome the past?

_____

_____

_____

_____

_____

_____

What do you enjoy doing that could help you cope with difficult times?

_____

_____

_____

_____

_____

_____

_____

_____

_____

_____

_____

_____

_____

Lesson 3: Learn to Survive

Lessons Learned: Advocacy takes courage. Have faith, stay strong and determined and you can survival and do extremely well.

Harriet survived the injury that crushed her skull and resulted in a life- long suffering from sleep spells. Today this is called narcolepsy.

This illness strengthened her commitment to change her life. She became determined to change her destiny. In changing her own life, she changed the lives of many others.

There are often drastic incidences that become life-changing experiences. Sometimes being an advocate for others is born out of your experiences, or of what you've observed happening to others.

Discussion: questions:

What trials have you had that made you stronger or more determined?

_____

_____

_____

_____

_____

_____

_____

_____

_____

How can you use difficulty in your life to motivate yourself and others?

_____

_____

_____

_____

_____

_____

_____

_____

_____

_____

_____

_____

_____

_____

_____

_____

_____

_____

_____

_____

_____

_____

_____

Lesson 4: Have a Support System

Lesson Learned: Develop positive relationships. Be supportive to others, accept support from others.

Harriet Tubman's extended family gave her support.
Everyone needs someone that he or she can call family. This is why people join clubs, churches, and gangs and develop other relationships. People need supportive people. The support from family, friends, or a group of like-minded people provides many chances for growth. Strong relationships make you stronger through hard times. Positive relationships build character and a strong spirit. Avoid negative or unhelpful relationships; they can lead to destruction of your spirit. Take some time to think about who you have to support you.

Discussion questions:

Who are the positive people in your life?

_____

_____

_____

_____

_____

_____

_____

_____

What can you do to show your support to others?

Lesson 5: Be Able to Communicate

Your ability to communicate well can make the difference in the outcome you seek.

Learn to use verbal and non- verbal forms of communication.

Be creative.

Harriet Tubman was also able to communicate with people outside of her own group. She learned new words from her educated friends.

She was able to communicate in two cultures.

There are differences in people's culture and education that influences their ability to understand each other. Nobody follows someone that he or she can't understand. A leader must have a special way of connecting. Sometime you can't convey in words the message you want to relay. Just like in a text message, friends have their own short hand and special language.

This is the same as what Harriet used. Songs were her "text messages."

Discussion questions:

What are some special words, jesters, or expression you use that only a few people in your core group/business setting understand?

_____

_____

_____

_____

_____

_____

How well are you able to communicate with those outside of your group?

_____

_____

_____

_____

_____

_____

_____

_____

_____

_____

Do you feel a need to improve your communication skills with those inside and outside of your core group? What do you need to do to start this process?

_____

_____

_____

_____

_____

_____

_____

_____

Lesson 6: On the Job Training

> **Learn from all experiences and keep a positive attitude.**
> **Stay optimistic, and have a sense of humor.**
> **Never give up your self-respect.**
>
> Harriet Tubman's life lessons started early. Sometimes life lessons are hard and even cruel.
> You might not realize at the time, but each day is a learning experience that is a resource for developing your personal goals and leadership style. Those lessons include learning the difference between the right way to treat people and the wrong way.

Discussion questions:

What types of tasks can you list that you have performed in school, in the community and in your jobs?

_____

_____

_____

_____

_____

_____

_____

_____

What is Optimism? Are you an optimist or pessimist?

PART TWO: LOOK TO THE FUTURE

Draw Your Future

Lesson 7: Be Determined

Determination will keep you going. It can also be the motivation for your actions. Advocacy requires dedication and commitment, giving your trust and keeping your word.

Harriet Tubman set her goals high. She risked her life numerous times to help those who wanted to be free. She knew that, to achieve her goals, she needed the help of others. She gave them her trust and she would not jeopardize that trusting relationship. Her sincerity in her mission made all necessary means of escape acceptable to her. This may seem a little extreme and possibly questionable in terms of her ethics. However, it was her style and it is all of our personal style that makes us human. There are no perfect humans. Remember, she felt she was on a mission from God.

Like Harriet, trust God and never doubt that you will succeed with every goal you set. "Let go and Let God." Have all confidence in your success under his control.

Discussion questions:

What are some examples of how your determination helped you achieve a goal?

_____

_____

_____

_____

_____

_____

What are some ways to use that same determination in other areas of your life?

Lesson 8: Realize the Goal with Others

Value of relationship.
Let love and compassion be your motivation for success.
Blessings are to be shared.

Harriet Tubman felt that freedom without someone to share it with will not
bring lasting joy. Family is important to your success.
You may reach the goal, but that is not the real source of happiness.
Being with people, you love and who love you, is the source of the joy.
God gives you people because we need each other.
God blesses us to be blessings to others.

Discussion questions:

**When you visualize your dreams, who do you have included in your
plan?**

_____

_____

_____

_____

_____

_____

_____

_____

How will you share your blessings?

Lesson 9: Dedicate Your Life to Your Passion

> **Show that you are responsible.**
> **Have compassion, and always pray.**
> **Be willing to make sacrifices.**
> **Help people build self-esteem and self-respect.**
>
> When Harriet Tubman committed her life to helping others, she kept focused on this goal, which was to take care of the needs of others. She did not stop. She was challenged, she may have grown weary and she was not healthy herself. Yet, she accepted the responsibility that comes with leadership and her plan was to fulfill her commitment as a lifelong duty.
> If you have a commitment to empower others, start by encouraging them. Stay focused on that goal.

Discussion questions:

What does it take to be truly dedicated to a cause?

_____

_____

_____

_____

_____

_____

_____

Do you know anyone who is an example of dedication to his or her passion? Who? What have they done? If so, study their life story.

_____

_____

_____

_____

_____

_____

_____

_____

_____

_____

_____

_____

_____

_____

_____

_____

_____

_____

_____

_____

_____

_____

_____

_____

_____

Lesson 10: Believe Dreams and Predictions

Can Become Reality

Be brave and have a passionate vision for your life.
Hold on to your dreams; know where you want to go.
With a sense of direction, your vision will come true.

In Harriet Tubman's time, it was ridiculous for a third generation slave to think that freedom was possible. The difference between Harriet Tubman and many other slaves that never tried to run away was courage. She wasn't afraid to dream big. She was not afraid to believe that she deserved to have a better life. It was her right.
She wanted freedom so bad she could see it, feel it and hear it.
Later, she realized it.
Don't be afraid to dream the impossible. Nothing is impossible.

Discussion questions:

What do you dream of doing?

_____

_____

_____

_____

_____

_____

_____

_____

What does your dream look like, sound like and feel like?

Lesson 11: Have a Sense of Humor

Keep your sense of humor.

Harriet Tubman used stories, songs, or jokes to decrease the stress and anxiety of her passengers. Stress can block the creativity and logical thinking.

Being able to make people laugh is a universal tool for making a positive connection.

Humor breaks the ice, personalizes an encounter, and builds relationships. Finding some humor in life is a powerful leadership skill.

Discussion questions:

What makes you laugh?

_____

_____

_____

_____

_____

_____

_____

_____

_____

_____

How do you feel after a good laugh?

How can you learn through humor?

Lesson 12: Listen and Learn

Develop your listening skills.

Seek to increase the diversity and cultural exchange in your group of friends. This leads to more equality, respect, and informed decisions.

Harriet Tubman was not formally educated, but she was smart.

She knew how to be an active listener.

Education is powerful and life changing. Listening and hearing are the same, but different. Hearing does not necessarily mean understanding what you hear. When you are listening, there is a process of interpretation in order to understand the message.

Active listening involves questioning what you heard, getting more information and being able to respond with an exchange of ideals.

Discussion questions:

Are you an active listener?

_____

_____

_____

_____

_____

_____

_____

_____

_____

Have you learned to talk less and listen more?

_____

_____

_____

_____

_____

How do you become a better, active listener?

_____

_____

_____

_____

_____

Would someone listening to you say that you respect others that
are different than you? What would they hear you say about
others?

_____

_____

_____

_____

_____

_____

_____

Lesson 13: Practice Financial Planning

Financial goals demand some sacrifice.

Harriet Tubman was able to use the little money she had to support her mission.

Learn to be thrifty and do with less today in order to do more tomorrow.

Hard work pays off. Be thrifty and plan for the future, be a goal setter.

Money can make a difference, but it's not everything.

Discussion questions:

Do you have a savings account? If not, why not?

_____

_____

_____

_____

_____

_____

_____

_____

_____

_____

_____

Are there things you can delay or sacrifice to decrease spending
and save more? List them here.

PART THREE: STRATEGIC PLANNING

Start your plan for the future: Where will you be on your progress towards your goal in 1 year, 5, years, 10 years?

_____

_____

_____

_____

_____

_____

_____

_____

_____

_____

_____

_____

_____

_____

_____

_____

_____

_____

_____

_____

_____

_____

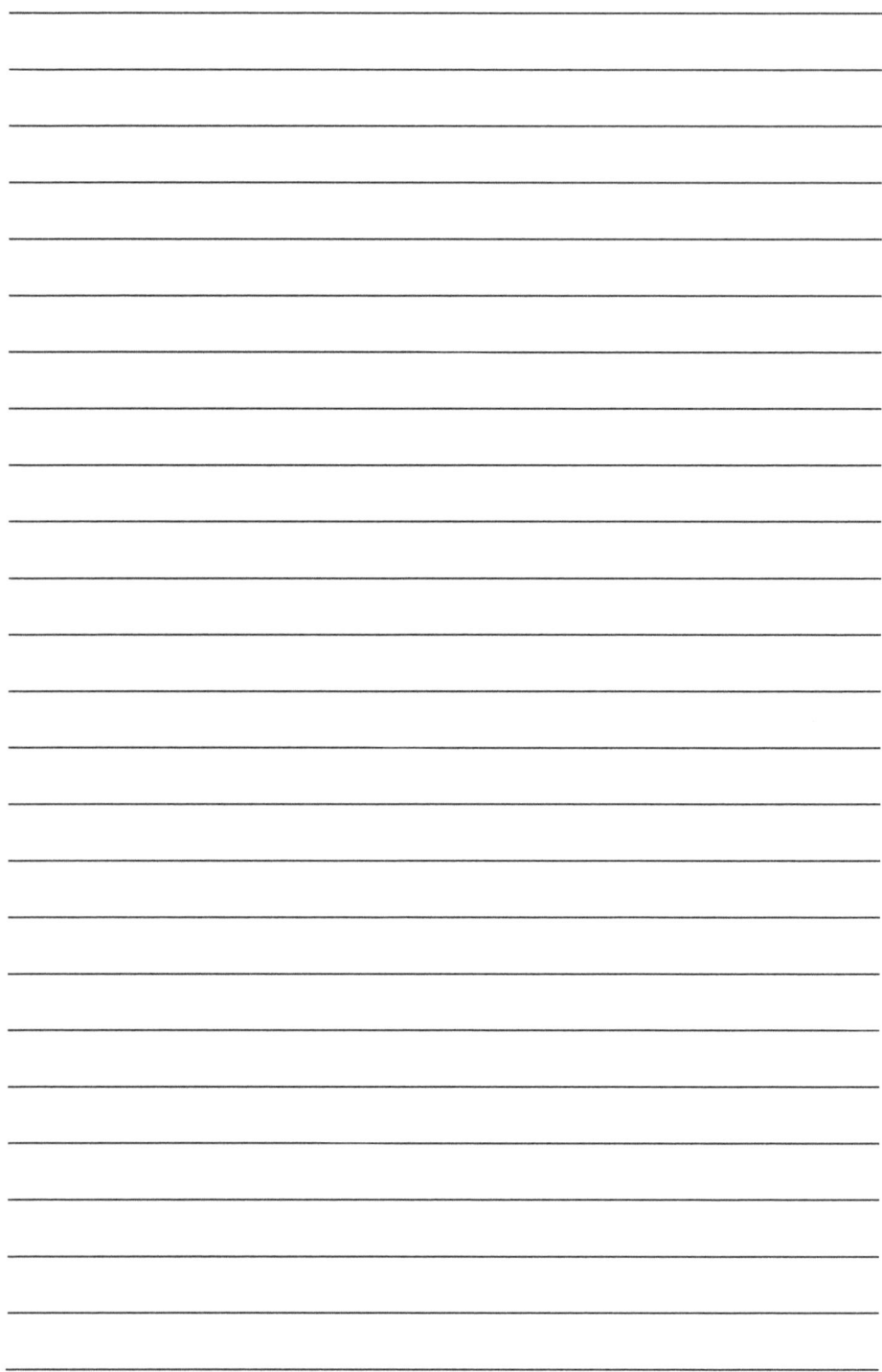

Lesson 14: Have Faith

Have faith, never give up, and follow your feeling, it could be God talking to you.

Harriet Tubman knew God on a personal level. She believed he would take care of her and she did not hesitate to follow God's directions.

Faith kept her going, and it was her faith that allowed her to overcome obstacles and the negative comments from those with less faith.

Often, you are the only one that holds onto the faith that you can accomplish your goals.

Hold on, you might have to change your route, but don't let fear stop you from reaching your goals.

Discussion questions:

How do you define faith?

_____

_____

_____

_____

_____

_____

_____

_____

Look up some definitions of faith. Can you list some that you can identify with and keep in your mind at all times?

_____

_____

_____

_____

_____

_____

_____

_____

_____

_____

_____

_____

_____

_____

_____

_____

_____

_____

_____

_____

_____

_____

_____

_____

Lesson 15: Stay Flexible

Be flexible, hold on to your faith.
Be compassionate and resourceful.

Harriet Tubman's love and determination kept her going back for
her sister. She did not grow cold and heartless with the heartbreak
of loosing her sister. Instead, she transferred the compassion to others.
Many things can factor into the journey toward a goal.
Don't be so focused or narrow-minded that only one outcome will
be acceptable.
You should always have an alternate route to your goal, or be ready to
make up a new plan on the spot.

Discussion questions:

How do you react when there is a change in your plans?

_____

_____

_____

_____

_____

_____

_____

_____

How do you practice being more flexible?

Lesson 16: Volunteer

Transferable skills are useful in all types of service to others.

Harriet Tubman used her skills she developed in one area in many ways.
Whenever you are learning by doing, these skills are useful in all that you do.
When you volunteer, the services you provide are important to those that
are receiving your support.
Nothing you do for others is a waste of time. Your payment may not be
in dollars, but you will gain benefits through volunteering.

Discussion questions:

**Have you thought of volunteering as another way to move towards
your goals?**

_____

_____

_____

_____

_____

_____

_____

_____

_____

_____

What can you do for an hour or two a week to help someone else?

Whenever you can travel. Appreciate nature, and enrich the life experience by meeting new people, seeing new places, trying new foods.

While traveling as Harriet Tubman, I have met many people I would have never met. I have learned more history about the state I live in just by visiting the libraries and schools around the state. I have many more great acquaintances and some new friends. It is through finding out about other places that you can evaluate your own environment.
Maybe there is a better place for you, or maybe you will learn to appreciate where you are even more.

Discussion questions:

Where would you go if you could go anywhere in the world?

_____

_____

_____

_____

_____

_____

_____

_____

_____

Can you identify places you would like to travel to and are willing to take the time to find out something about before your visit?

_____

_____

_____

_____

_____

_____

_____

_____

_____

_____

_____

Have you visited this location vicariously? (By reading a book, visiting a website, or watching a travel show).

_____

_____

_____

_____

_____

_____

_____

_____

_____

Lesson 18: Learn to Tell and Write Your Stories

Oral communication is important, telling stories is a natural way we talk.

Harriet Tubman told her stories that we call oral history. If her stories were not written, we would not know as much about her as we do today.

To make history, stories should be written down.

Storytelling stimulates your mind by making learning more interesting. Interesting learning leads to growth.

Read stories, and write and tell your own stories.

Share your stories with others.

Discussion questions:

What is your story? How can you draw upon personal moments to help others? Are you willing to write something about yourself that you would like recorded in history?

_____

_____

_____

_____

_____

_____

_____

_____

_____

_____

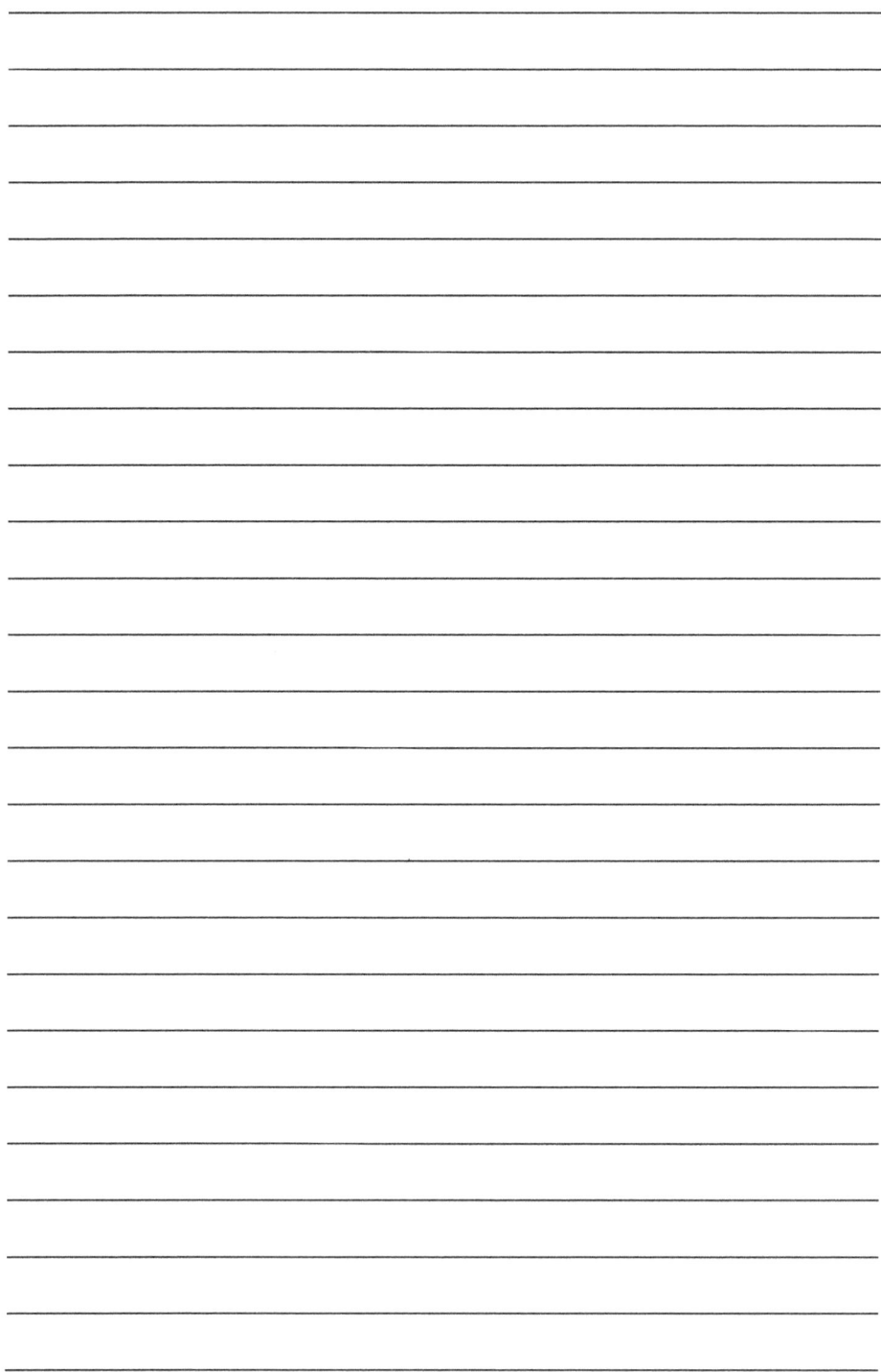

Lesson 19: Find Mentors

Seek out knowledge from other people.
Learn from your own and other people's experiences.

Harriet Tubman took advantage of opportunities to learn from other people. She never learned to read or write, but this didn't stop her from increasing her knowledge.

Don't be afraid to associate with people with more education or people who are different than you. Most people are willing to share their knowledge with others. It is up to those wanting to learn to find someone with the information you would like to know and to listen to them.

Discussion questions:

What do you want to learn more about?

_____

_____

_____

_____

_____

_____

_____

_____

_____

_____

Is it important enough to you to take time to list some resources where you can find this information? If yes, Start now.

_____

_____

_____

_____

_____

_____

_____

_____

Who do you know that knows something about this topic? Maybe it is someone you know that is associated with someone else with the information.

_____

_____

_____

_____

_____

_____

_____

_____

_____

_____

_____

Lesson 20: Learn a Little Politics

> **Lesson Learned: Respect earns respect; Politics is people and power. Know the names of the powerful people and study their politics.**
>
> Harriet Tubman did what she was compassionate about. When you show your compassion, people respect what you do.
> Others with similar beliefs and causes will be drawn to you.
> People who work together have power.
> Synergy is a great word. It means working together to get greater
> Results than working alone. This is what politics is about, people using their power by working together to influence the government affairs.
> Get involved and make a difference.

Discussion questions:

What issues or a causes concern you?

_____

_____

_____

_____

_____

_____

_____

_____

_____

How can you work with others to strengthen your power to make change on what you are concerned about?

PART FOUR: DON'T FORGET WHERE YOU CAME FROM

Draw a picture of where did you came from.

Lesson 21: Learn to Network

Lesson Learned: Networking is being social and building relationships.

Harriet Tubman had friends that introduced her to their friends. These connections provided opportunities she would have never found by herself. Respectful relationships build strong networks. If you ever need a reference, the relationships you have built will benefit you greatly. Remember never to burn your bridges.

In other words, don't leave a relationship with bad feelings. You never know when you need to call on someone to say something good for you.

Discussion questions:

Whom can you ask to write you a letter of reference?

_____

_____

_____

_____

_____

_____

_____

_____

_____

What do you think they will say about you?

Lesson 22: Be Humble

Be humble and willing to serve others. Pray and give God the glory.

Harriet Tubman was a very humble person, she found no shame in being who she was and doing the work she did. Humility is not the same as humiliation, which is shame and embarrassment. Being humble is feeling or showing respect and admiration toward other people. Being humble also means giving service and taking responsibility for others needs and comforts before your own.

It is a demonstration of being of higher rather than a lower level of character. There is greatness not weakness in humility.

Discussion question:

How is being humble showing greatness?

_____

_____

_____

_____

_____

_____

_____

_____

_____

Are there people that you can name whom are examples of being humble that you admire? What do they do to show humility?

_____

_____

_____

_____

_____

_____

_____

_____

_____

_____

_____

_____

_____

_____

_____

_____

_____

_____

_____

_____

_____

_____

_____

Lesson 23: Build a Strong Team

Teambuilding involves diversity, recognition and appreciation, shared decisions making and recruitment of skillful people.

As skillful as Harriet Tubman was, she could not do everything by herself.

Teams help leaders reach their goals. The strength of a team is diversity. When you're able to work with people with different skill sets and from different cultures, you get better results.

Discussion questions:

What do you bring to the team?

_____

_____

_____

_____

_____

_____

_____

_____

_____

_____

_____

_____

_____

What processes are important to keep a team working well together?

Lesson 24: Support Women

Seek women for comradeship, support, joint efforts and advocacy, and as mentors.

Harriet Tubman was a woman of action and she sought out other women to work towards improving life in American for everyone.

Women are strong and when dedicated to a cause, they are unstoppable. Women can and should work toward supporting each other. Older more mature women are important in the development in self-esteem and leadership younger women.

Discussion questions:

Name some women in your life that you feel are great leaders.

_____

_____

_____

_____

_____

_____

_____

_____

_____

_____

_____

_____

What are some of the traits these women demonstrate that make them great leaders?

_____

_____

_____

_____

_____

_____

_____

_____

What are some of these traits that you share with these great leaders?

_____

_____

_____

_____

_____

_____

_____

_____

_____

_____

_____

_____

_____

Lesson 25: Bring Others Up

Lesson Learned: Share your blessings and be dedicated to helping others. Love, compassion, community, and responsibility are valuable tools for taking actions.

Harriet Tubman went back to bring others up to a better life. There were about three thousand known conductors on the Underground Railroad. Some of those conductors were ex-slaves who could not enjoy freedom knowing those they left behind were suffering. Seek to help others achieve what you have, or more. Remember we are blessed to bless others.

Discussion questions:

Who are the people; family, teachers, and friends you can list that have helped you along the way?

_____

_____

_____

_____

_____

_____

_____

_____

_____

_____

What can you do to bring someone up to a better place?

Lesson 26: Teach Others to Do for Themselves

Lesson Learned: Be caring and empower others.

Harriet Tubman knew she could not be everywhere and do everything her people needed. She did know that these people were smart, and if given instructions, they could do what they needed to do for themselves.

Being able to empower someone is to give them the power in the way of education or motivation to do something for themselves.

This gift keeps on giving.

Discussion question:

What do you know that you can teach someone else to do?

_____

_____

_____

_____

_____

_____

_____

_____

_____

_____

_____

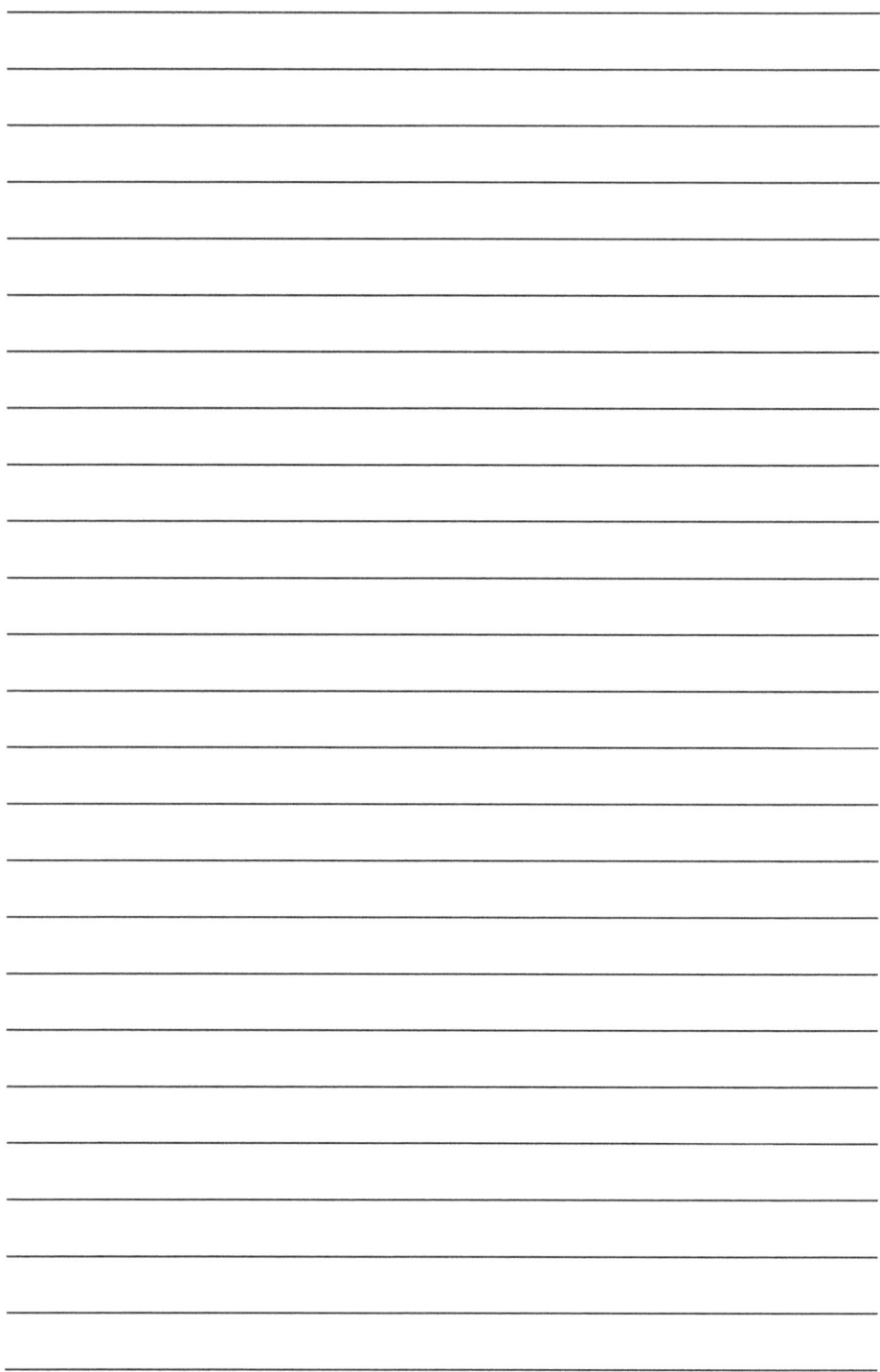

Lesson 27: Take Action When Needed

Advocate for others means to take actions and stand for what you believe.

Harriet Tubman saved this man from being returned to slavery. Before she took actions, there was only talk about the situation. She took the leadership role to bring the necessary action needed.

Advocating for others is hard to do. Sometimes it requires you to put yourself at some risk. If you step out and speak out for someone else, you are now taking on the same problem or looked at the same as they are. If you feel strongly about something that seems wrong, take some actions. Actions speak louder than words. You could be the one that makes a difference.

Discussion questions:

What organization have you heard about that fits the definition of advocacy, (to support, campaign, sponsor, and believe in someone or something)?

_____

_____

_____

_____

_____

_____

_____

Is there anything you would be willing to advocate for?

Lesson 28: Be Willing to Make Some Sacrifices

Lesson Learned: Relationships are built on trust.

Harriet Tubman's love for all people and her willingness to serve meant that she had to earn the trust of the people she wanted to help.

Service to others may require sacrifices, you have to earn trust.

When you're faced with the same or similar situation, will you be willing to sacrifice finances and/or comfort in order to reach the goal?

Discussion question:

What will you give up for someone you love?

_____

_____

_____

_____

_____

_____

_____

_____

_____

_____

_____

How do you show people that you are trustworthy?

Lesson 29: Have Courage and Don't Be Afraid To Speak Up

> **Have courage. Speak up for yourself and others.**
> **Take a stance, claim your rights, and demand your respect.**
>
> Harriet Tubman was a storyteller. A simple parable can express more than a statement made in anger. She had too much self-respect to let someone else determine her life.
> Don't let others decide your fate without you giving them your thoughts.
> Don't be afraid to speak in simple language.
> Use your own style of communication. It may be through a stories, songs, or poetry that expresses your deepest feelings.
> Your creative message may be the best way for people to understand how you and many others feel. Being yourself is the best way to get the results you want.

Discussion question:

There is more than one way to make your voice heard. Can you list some ways you can be a spokesperson?

_____

_____

_____

_____

_____

_____

_____

_____

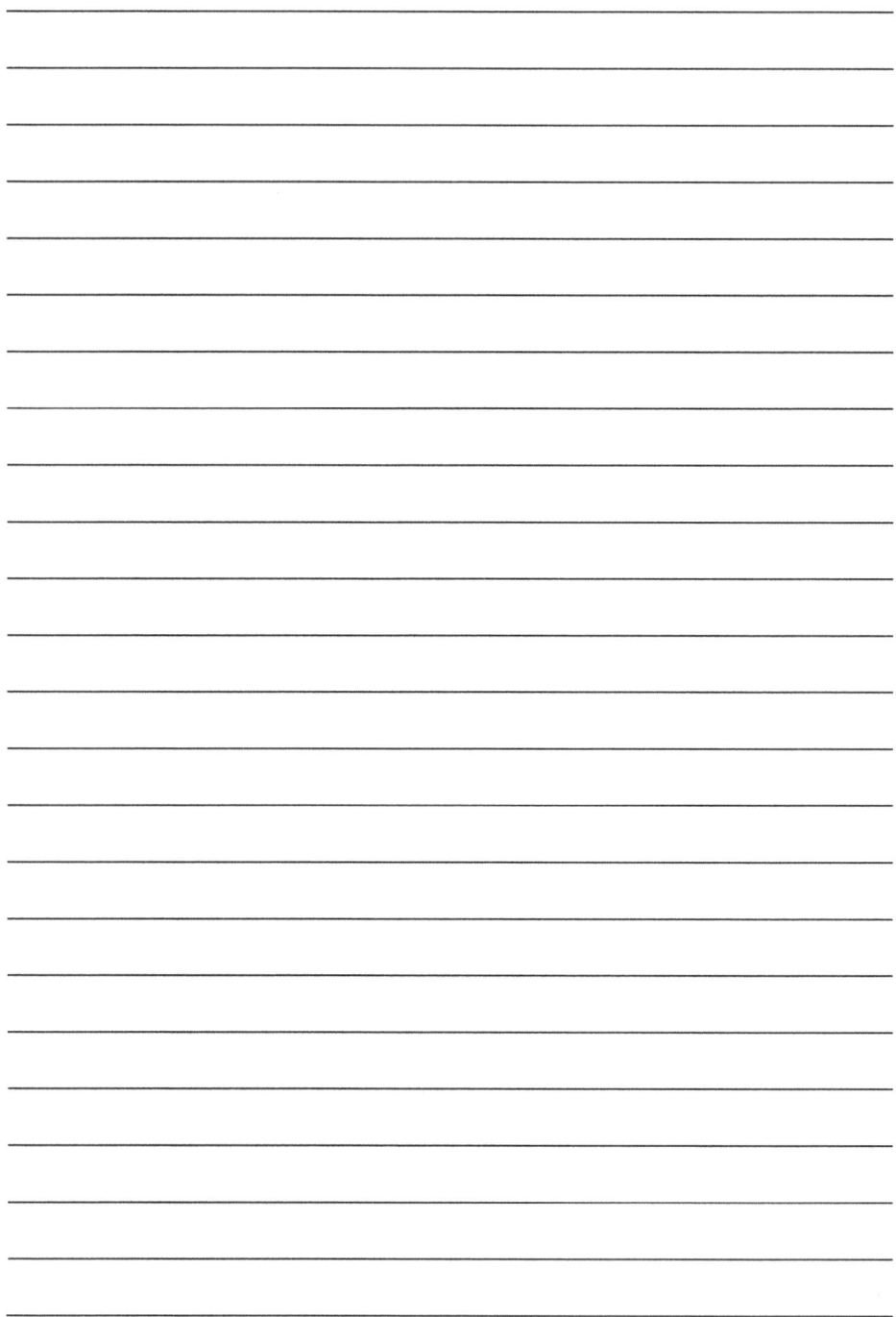

Lesson 30: Be Grateful

Express your Gratefulness to God and be modest.

Harriet Tubman provided examples of how she communicated with God.
She never took credit for doing anything herself. She felt any help that came
to her, came from God. She trusted him and thanked him for all he did. She
listened to his voice in different ways.

This is her intuition, the fast heartbeats, and a small voice in the head
telling her which way to go. Be grateful and look and listen to God speaking
to you.

Remember to thank Him for what you have, what he has done for you, and
what he is doing for you everyday.

Discussion question:

What are you grateful for? _____

_____

_____

_____

_____

_____

_____

_____

What can you do to develop an attitude of gratitude?

What can you do to show that you appreciate people in your life?

PART FIVE: PLANT YOUR SEEDS

Lesson Learned: Leave a Legacy

Educate your mind to be free.

The stories of Harriet Tubman's stories presented in this book are documented history. Think about her life- what the stories tell you about her love for others, her leadership skills, and the legacy she left.

She was born a slave in 1820. There was nothing anyone could see that was special about her. Harriet was not beautiful or educated, but she found a way to keep going until she reached her goals.

I hope you are encouraged by Harriet Tubman to follow your dreams. As Harriet planted apple seeds, you can use this information to plant seeds in your life and that of others. What I mean by planting your seeds is making plans for your future. You can't have the apples, peaches or pears without first having the seeds to plant that will grow into the tree.

Goal setting in your life is the same as planting those seeds. You have to decide what you want. Apple seeds will not give you peaches, pears, or plums, only apples. You may be smart, good looking, and a fast talker, but without taking the right actions, you won't reach your goal of becoming a better student, successful businessperson, or even a healthier person.

As a young girl, Harriet Tubman couldn't imagine that one day people would write about her and one hundred years after her death, people around the world would know her name and build statues in her honor.

It was never about fame and fortune for her; it was about following a dream. Freedom for herself and her people was her dream, and she dedicated her life to making it come true. It is only because she would not give up on this dream that we know her name today.

Do what you dream of doing after the example of Harriet Tubman; with love. Take the lead to help other people, and you will leave a legacy. We will all one day leave this world. But, will we do anything as individuals that will leave the world any better for someone we leave behind?

When you have an insurance policy so that your children and family are taken care of when you are gone, that is considered leaving a legacy. Please bear in mind that a legacy is not just a matter of your immediate family.

Remember, apples are ready to buy in the stores today, but where did those apples come from? Someone had to plant the seeds. Everyone can do something they can be proud of, that people will remember.

That is your legacy. There are many ways to make a lasting contribution to the world while we are living that can leave a legacy, a lasting memory and honor. **I present to you the stories of Harriet Tubman to show you the power of one, anyone. Even YOU.**

Send me an email at: karol@harriettubmanbooks.com and share how Harriet Tubman has touched your life.

Visit my website for resources on Harriet Tubman and on developing your leadership skills. www.harriettubmanbooks.com

Karol V. Brown

Your reflections:

www.ingramcontent.com/pod-product-compliance
Lightning Source LLC
Chambersburg PA
CBHW020950030426
42339CB00004B/39